IMAGES
of Rail

STEAMTOWN NATIONAL HISTORIC SITE

ON THE COVER: This image is reminiscent of days gone by on the old Delaware, Lackawanna & Western (DL&W) Railroad. The 19th-century rail yard would later become the home of the Steamtown National Historic Site. DL&W Engine No. 936 4-4-0 was built in 1911. (Steamtown National Historic Site, National Park Service Archives.)

IMAGES
of Rail

STEAMTOWN NATIONAL HISTORIC SITE

Margo L. Azzarelli
Foreword by Ruth Giardina

ARCADIA
PUBLISHING

Published by Arcadia Publishing
Charleston, South Carolina

Printed in the United States of America

Library of Congress Control Number: 2020933017

For all general information, please contact Arcadia Publishing:
Telephone 843-853-2070
Fax 843-853-0044
E-mail sales@arcadiapublishing.com
For customer service and orders:
Toll-Free 1-888-313-2665

Visit us on the Internet at www.arcadiapublishing.com

This book is dedicated to the memory of Susan Morningstar, the first female railroad employee, hired in 1851 by the Baltimore & Ohio Railroad.

CONTENTS

FOREWORD

"I wish I had come here years ago!" This is one of the most frequent comments that we hear at Steamtown National Historic Site. People from all 50 states and scores of other countries pass through this park every year. Some are devoted national park visitors, some are railroad fans, and many just want to experience a part of America's past. Virtually all first-time visitors are astounded by how much there is to see, learn, and experience. In 1986, the National Park Service began rehabilitating over 60 acres in Scranton, Pennsylvania, that were once the home of the Delaware, Lackawanna & Western Railroad. Long-abandoned buildings and tracks were replaced with working rails, as well as a beautiful history and technology museum. Of course, the locomotives are the best part of the site. Starting with the generous donation of a private collection, Steamtown later acquired other unique locomotives and cars and countless other railroad artifacts. Steamtown preserves and celebrates an era of American history that was essential to its cultural, industrial, and economic growth. I am delighted that my good friend Margo Azzarelli has taken on the enormous challenge of writing a concise history of this remarkable site. In this, Margo's eighth book, she continues to share her vast knowledge of the history of the Lackawanna Valley and its people. I have witnessed her tireless commitment to thoroughly researching all aspects of Steamtown's growth. It is my hope that this book will inspire readers to visit Steamtown National Historic Site and all of our precious national parks to enjoy these treasures for years to come.

—Ruth Giardina

ACKNOWLEDGMENTS

I would like to thank my family and friends for their support on this project, especially my favorite scanner and daughter, Marnie Azzarelli. A special thank-you is owed to the staff and crew at Steamtown National Historic Site for all their help, including Cheri Shepherd, Richard "Pat" McKnight, Ruth Giardina, John Mucha, Chris LaBar, Sara LaBar, Tim O'Malley, Kathryn Lang, Flor Blum, Lori Staely, Peter Millett, Bill Fischer, and Will Eukulenko. My gratitude also goes out to all the train historians and photographers, past and present, who contributed to this book: Thomas T. Tabor, Watson Bunnell, Ed Miller, Don Ball, Gordon Chapell, Kenny Ganz, D.M. Crispino, Jim Boyd, Dennis A. Livesey, David Morrison, Bob Harris, and John Hart. A special shout-out to Angel Hisnanick for her help and patience!

Unless otherwise noted, all images appear courtesy of the Steamtown National Historic Site, National Park Service Archives.

INTRODUCTION

John Fitch is a name many may not recognize. Back in the 18th century, Fitch lived in a log cabin in Kentucky. He was not a man of wealth, but it is said that he invented the first steam locomotive, during the 1780s. It is considered to be the oldest in the world. It was only a couple feet wide and not very long. Fitch found his way to Philadelphia and had the honor of demonstrating his locomotive to George Washington and his cabinet. Today, it is on display in the Ohio Historical Society Museum. Unfortunately for Fitch, his invention was quickly forgotten, and he died of alcoholism in 1799. The steam locomotive would not take hold until rich Englishman Richard Trevithick came into the picture with his own invention. Trevithick had the means and the methods that Fitch lacked, and he would be given the credit for inventing the first steam locomotive to run on wheels.

Steam railroading first developed in Great Britain, where engineering and industrialization were years ahead of the United States. But things would soon change.

In 1840, George and Seldon Scranton (for whom the city is named), along with Sanford Grant, purchased 503 acres of land, and the construction of the first blast furnace began. At first, the company was unable to profit from making iron nails because of their poor quality. At the time, the railroads were expanding, and George Scranton advised his brother: "We must begin to think about making R.R. Iron T rail." In 1846, the Scrantons negotiated a deal with the New York & Erie (NY&E) Railroad to manufacture and deliver 12,000 tons of wrought iron T-rails in order to complete its track to Binghamton by December 31, 1848, or the NY&E would lose a large state subsidy. This risky business endeavor saved both companies.

"We have now proven that we can make iron with hard coal, the next thing we have to prove is that we can make a profit out of it," said George Scranton—and profit they did.

In 1849, the Scranton Company purchased the charter of the Leggett's Gap Railroad, the first proposed rail line in the Lackawanna Valley. Although chartered many years prior, construction on the route over Moosic Mountain via Clarks Summit to Great Bend had never begun. Ground was broken in 1850 with a track gauge of six feet to facilitate interchange with the Erie Railroad at Great Bend. The Scranton brothers formed the Delaware, Lackawanna & Western Railroad from the merger of three other railroads, the Cayuga & Susquehanna, the Lackawanna & Western (former Leggett's Gap), and the Delaware & Cobb's Gap. It was also known as the "Lackawanna Railroad." At its height, the DL&W operated on about 1,000 miles of main line and branch track between Hoboken, New Jersey, and Buffalo, New York. The DL&W also purchased 28 acres of land from the Lackawanna Iron & Coal Company in 1853. This would be the genesis of the Scranton yard.

The DL&W was originally formed for the transportation of iron product from the furnaces to market. However, seeing the rise in demand for anthracite coal in the region, the Scrantons seized the financial opportunity and began to transport anthracite as well, until antimonopoly laws forced railroads to stop in 1921. Over the next several decades, many changes to the railroad industry would occur.

In May 1934, the age of steam came to a symbolic end when two stainless steel streamlined diesel-electric passenger engines were unveiled at Chicago's Century of Progress Exposition. By May 24 of that year, diesel passenger trains began regular service. As steam locomotives began to disappear, the DL&W kept up with the changing times by adding more and more diesel locomotives to its fleet. The fictional train *Phoebe Snow* symbolized Lackawanna's diesel age. By the late 1950s, travel by air became more prevalent than by train. To avoid bankruptcy, the DL&W merged with its longtime rival, the Erie Railroad, to become the Erie Lackawanna Railroad. But despite much efforts by many, railroads in the Northeast had collapsed by 1968. In 1972, Hurricane Agnes flooded over 135 miles of the Erie Lackawanna track in Pennsylvania and New York. This would be its final economic blow. When the company went bankrupt, it became part of the Consolidated Rail Corporation, and the Scranton yard was deeded to Conrail in 1976. After many years of neglect, the once productive and flourishing rail yard at the hub of the city fell into disrepair and was eventually abandoned.

Steamtown's collection of locomotives was started in the mid-1950s by seafood mogul Francis Nelson Blount, who was born in Warren, Rhode Island, in 1918. As a boy, Blount and his best friend Fred Richardson were so interested in steam locomotives that they wrote one of the very first railroading books, titled *Along the Iron Rails*.

Later in life, Blount became the president of the Blount Seafood Corporation. He remained an avid steam locomotive enthusiast, trained with the Boston & Maine Railroad to become an engineer, and enjoyed many other hobbies, which included deep-sea fishing and aviation.

After he purchased the narrow-gauge Edaville Railroad in South Carver, Massachusetts, in 1956, Blount began acquiring standard-gauge locomotives and railroad cars. Due to his growing collection of standard-gauge locomotives, and being that Edaville was a narrow-gauge railroad, he needed to find a new vicinity to store them. In 1960, he moved his collection to North Walpole, New Hampshire, where he had hoped to open a state railroad museum, but he did not get the support he needed from the State of New Hampshire for this endeavor. In 1964, Blount moved yet again, this time to the recently abandoned Rutland Railroad yard in Bellows Fall, Vermont, and the Steamtown Foundation for the Preservation of Steam and Railroad Americana, better known as Steamtown, USA, was born. Sadly, F. Nelson Blount did not get to enjoy the success of his nonprofit train museum; he tragically passed away in 1967 after crashing his small aircraft. Though many efforts were made to keep Steamtown, USA up and running, it would fall on hard financial times without Blount behind the helm. Eventually, a new home was needed for Blount's legacy. Thirty different communities threw their engineer hats into the ring, and Scranton, known for its railroading history, was chosen to become the new home of Steamtown, USA in 1980. But it would take another four years to get all the plans in place, and in 1984, Steamtown, USA finally began its move to the abandoned Delaware, Lackawanna & Western Railroad yard in Scranton. Unfortunately, Steamtown was not the financial success that the community had hoped for under private operation. Faced with bankruptcy and the possibility of losing its collection, Steamtown, USA went in search of funding. Pennsylvania congressman Joseph M. McDade lent a helping hand and made arrangements for William Penn Mott, director of the National Park Service, to visit the former DL&W yards. He found the idea of creating a railroad park on the site appealing. On October 30, 1986, the federal government took ownership of the collection with the establishment of the Steamtown National Historic Site, making it the only federally operated site of its kind.

Steamtown's mission statement sums it up nicely—to further public understanding and appreciation of the development of steam railroading and its culture in the United States, as well as to preserve, protect, and enhance the site's rolling stock and artifacts for future generations. Former Scranton mayor James Connors explains, "The people in this area created this history and now we're preserving it." The Steamtown National Historic Site will continue to do so for many years to come.

One

THE RAILROAD YARD

Pictured is the 1855 oil painting *The Lackawanna Valley* by George Inness. It depicts the future home of the Steamtown National Historic Site. The artist shows industry about to collide with agriculture. The well-known painting is displayed in the National Gallery of Art in Washington, DC.

The dream of George Scranton (left) was to have a depot full of freight all the time, waiting to be taken away. George Scranton and Seldon T. Scranton (below) were the founders of the Delaware, Lackawanna & Western Railroad, also known as the Lackawanna Railroad, in 1853. George's dream would soon come true. The DL&W provided a way of hauling its iron products, particularly T-rails used in the construction of railroads, to market. The company was also a major shipper of anthracite coal.

In the late 19th century, the Scranton yards were bustling with steam power. The Delaware, Lackawanna & Western No. 0083 4-4-0 was built in 1893.

Men are posing on the Delaware, Lackawanna & Western No. 0148 2-6-0, built in 1891. Because of the promise of employment on the railroads and in the coal mines, people of many different ethnicities would make their way from Ellis Island to Scranton.

So many of these beautiful trains have come and gone, like the DL&W No. 1052 4-6-0, which was built by Alco and Rogers in 1907. The only original DL&W locomotive that still remains at the site is the No. 565, which is on display in the roundhouse.

This view of the DL&W carshops is from the early 1900s. In 1851, the area was a meadow with both sheep and wolves roaming about. Once the Scrantons purchased the land to form the DL&W Scranton rail yard, trees were cut down and stone was blasted. It would take an estimated three years to develop a line to New York.

The Delaware, Lackawanna & Western Railroad built a series of roundhouses and turntables, shops, and other buildings between 1854 and 1937. When Steamtown became a historic site, a construction archeologist team was called in to study the buried foundation. The exterior wall of the original 1865 roundhouse and remnants of brick inspection pits had been discovered. The DL&W spent many years constructing and reconstructing, always striving for improvement in order to keep up with the competition. This photograph was taken around 1906.

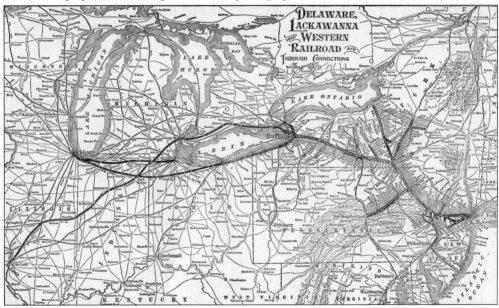

Early in the 1850s, the Scrantons' intentions when they formed the Delaware & Cobb's Gap Railroad were to connect the city and its industry to the Delaware River. But, in less than a decade, through construction, traffic agreements, leases, and the purchase of connecting lines, the DL&W grew a railroad system that connected Scranton with upstate New York and the Atlantic seaboard. The DL&W became a major shipper of anthracite and iron products and continued to grow. The cities along its route included Buffalo, Corning, Elmira, Syracuse, Utica, and Binghamton in New York; Northumberland, Bloomsburg, Scranton, East Stroudsburg, and Delaware Water Gap in Pennsylvania; and Phillipsburg, Newark, and Hoboken in New Jersey. (Courtesy of D.M. Crispino.)

Thomas Dickson (pictured) and his two brothers, John and George, organized the Dickson Manufacturing Company in 1862. The company purchased the Cliff Locomotive Works of Scranton from Cooke and Company of New York. The Cliff Locomotive Works site included buildings at the east end of the 200 block of Cliff Street, adjacent to the DL&W yard. The Dickson locomotive division operated under the name Dickson Locomotive Works. The first locomotive the company built was for the Delaware & Hudson Railroad and was named *Lackawanna*. In 1874, a fire heavily damaged the Dickson Locomotive Works erecting shop and destroyed other buildings at the Cliff Locomotive Works. It rebuilt the following year. In 1901, the Dickson Manufacturing Company was sold, and the Dickson Locomotive Works was acquired by the American Locomotive Company (ALCO). The new owner closed the Scranton shops in 1909. It moved to Schenectady and later went on to produce the 4-8-8-4 Union Pacific "Big Boy" in the 1940s.

In 1906, a 400-foot-long cinder pit was built next to the roundhouse with an overhead traveling crane. A 900-foot-long by 25-foot-wide coal trestle used for fueling the locomotives was also built. Before entering the roundhouse, a locomotive's fire had to be dumped out. The fireman would use a long-handled clinker rule to pull the ashes and burning cinders from beneath the fire grates. The contents of the ash pan were then dumped onto the ground between the rails or a water-filled cinder pit.

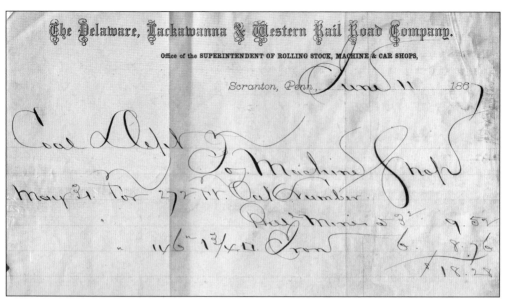

Dated 1867, this is a piece of paper history from the DL&W coal department, which handled both mining and sales. It was ranked fourth among anthracite producers in the 1870s. It is said that the DL&W was the best managed and most profitable of the anthracite roads under the tight-fisted administration of Samuel Sloan, president from 1867 to 1899.

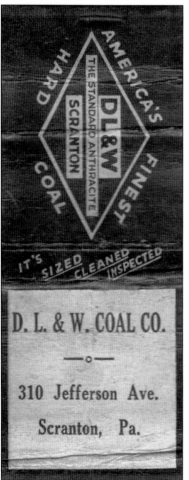

The offices of the DL&W coal department were located at 310 Jefferson Avenue in Scranton until the Sherman Antitrust Act separated anthracite railroads from coal-mining interests in 1921. DL&W would later sell its coal department to the Glen Alden Coal Company. (Courtesy of D.M. Crispino.)

In the summer of 1877, railroad companies cut their employee wages by 10 percent for the second time in 12 months. Furious with yet another wage cut, employees left their posts on the Baltimore & Ohio Railroad, and the trains abruptly stopped on July 16. The workers of the Pennsylvania Railroad and DL&W followed suit. The Great Railroad Strike spread across the nation, and two-thirds of the trains did not run. Riots broke out in many cities, including Scranton. Unfortunately, the workers gave in to the companies, and returned to work by the end of July without receiving the 10 percent that had been stolen from them by the owners. The wage cut and strike affected the coal industry as well; the miners also walked out of the mines. They returned in October without an increase in wages or better working conditions.

The superintendent of the DL&W coal department was initially Joseph Albright. After leaving the company to join the Delaware & Hudson, he was replaced by William Storrs; pictured is a letter sent to him by an associate. The DL&W had a direct advantage; it was allowed to operate coal mines. It began mining around 1851 when the coal department was organized.

The DL&W's first train station was on the corner of Lackawanna and Wyoming Avenues. In 1864, it was replaced by a Victorian-style brick station, which remained in use for 40 years. The 1864 station was later demolished to make way for its predecessor, a beautiful French Renaissance–style building that would be hailed as one of the most beautiful stations in the nation at the time.

Samuel Sloan (right) became DL&W's president in August 1867. While at the helm, he continued to make improvements by building and expanding the railroad's lines. During this time, anthracite reigned supreme as the primary fuel source in the East. Sloan's keen business mind knew that he had to expand the market for anthracite, and he strived to acquire additional mines. He remained in the position until 1899, when William Truesdale (below) took over. He was the man who brought much success to the DL&W with his innovative methods and major modernization programs. Many of the structures still standing today at the Steamtown National Historic Site are because of Truesdale, who remained as president until 1925.

East of Scranton is the Nay Aug Tunnel, which was on the main line of the DL&W. As part of the DL&W's modernization project, the tunnel was built in 1856, and its parallel tunnel, the south tunnel, was constructed in 1905. It consists of two bore holes through a hill. The tunnel sustained heavy damage in 1955 during Hurricane Diane, and the south tunnel has not been used since. The north side is currently active. These photographs were taken in 1906.

The Scranton Iron Furnaces, started by Seldon and George Scranton and Sanford Grant in 1840, was once a great source of revenue for the city until the company moved its operations to Lackawanna, New York, in 1902. Pictured are remnants of the iron furnaces.

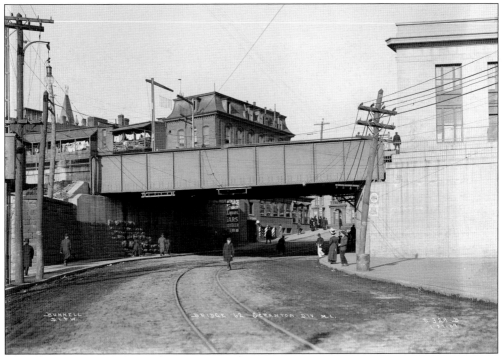

Bridge No. 62 was erected by the DL&W after the turn of the 20th century. It carried passenger and freight traffic and is located across Cedar Avenue near the historic Scranton Iron Furnaces.

The DL&W had a new coal trestle constructed in 1906 adjacent to the ash handling facilities. It included two sand hoppers used for various service needs on locomotives simultaneously. The coal trestle in the Scranton yard supplied coal to locomotives operating on the road's main line as well as in the yards. Trestles held both anthracite and soft coal in various sizes. It ceased operation when the railroad completed its conversion to diesel engines in the early 1950s. It was demolished in 1950. Today, all that remains of the structure are the concrete foundation and ramp.

Pictured is the site of what would become the home of the DL&W's new passenger terminal and offices.

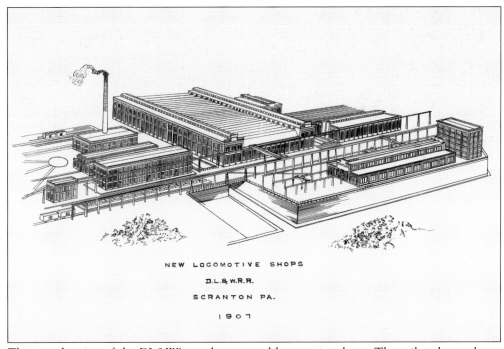

NEW LOCOMOTIVE SHOPS

D.L.& W.R.R.

SCRANTON PA.

1907

This is a drawing of the DL&W's newly proposed locomotive shops. The railroad was always building and improving, particularly under the Truesdale administration. Construction would not begin until 1907, and completion would take two years.

This photograph of the locomotive yard in 1908 gives a good view of its many impressive buildings. In 1902, the original 1855 roundhouse near Washington Avenue was removed. The 1865 roundhouse was also torn down, and a larger 46-stall roundhouse was built in its place. The machine shop also received renovations and new paint.

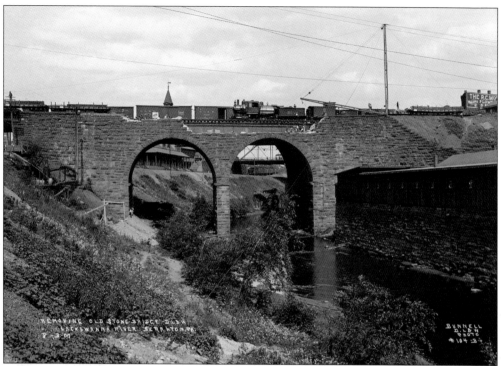

In 1907, workers began to remove the old stone from what was then called the Lackawanna River Bridge, also known as Bridge No. 60, at the west end of the Scranton yard. The new bridge they were planning to build would be the third one in this location.

Here, a new steel bridge is being built to replace its old stone predecessor. Its construction is typical of DL&W plate girder and concrete railroad bridges at the turn of the 20th century. Bridge No. 60 crosses the Lackawanna River, and it controlled traffic between the yards and the DL&W's main line and Bloomsburg branch.

In 1907, the DL&W hired New Jersey architect Frank J. Niles to replace the original locomotive shops. The foundry was built at the present site of General Dynamics Works on Cedar Avenue, where the Lackawanna Iron and Steel Company's rolling and steel mills once stood. The foundry is where castings are produced by melting metal, pouring liquid into a mold, and allowing it time to solidify.

The construction of the erecting shop began in 1907 and was completed in 1909. In this shop, heavy maintenance was done on the locomotives. Over 70 locomotives were built in the facility. The building also includes a foundry, blacksmith shop, machine shop, and a laboratory. The DL&W sold this part of the facility in 1951 to the government. At the time, 1,300 men were employed in the shops.

The pattern shop is another of the notable buildings at the former Scranton Army Ammunition Plant. The area for making the wooden patterns was on the ground floor, and the patterns were stored on the upper four floors. The lumber was received and kept in the basement. Unlike the other shop buildings, the pattern shop was built on a reinforced concrete frame for fireproofing due to the large amount of lumber stored there. Construction began in 1907, and the building was completed in 1909.

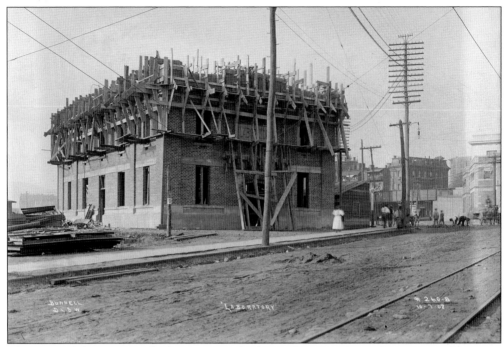

The DL&W laboratory was built in 1908 at the former Scranton Army Ammunition Plant site, which is presently General Dynamics Works on Cedar Avenue.

In 1909, the office and storage building was constructed. At the time, it was used as a warehouse for the erection shop across South Washington Avenue. The two buildings were connected by an underground electric tram. It also served as the main office for the Scranton yard. Today, it is the superintendent and administration building of the Steamtown National Historic Site.

The gashouse of the DL&W was constructed in 1909 and put into operation in 1910. Its purpose was to supply fuel to the foundries and furnaces of the locomotive shops at the site. It was designed by architect Frank J. Nies under supervision of chief engineer Lincoln Bush as a two-story building with room to hold three to five employees. A year after the gashouse opened, it was proclaimed a complete success, having provided a dependable source of efficient and economical fuel to the shops. During the diesel era of the 1950s and 1960s, the building was used as a machine shop. It remains today on South Washington Avenue.

During the period when the erecting shops were constructed, they were considered ahead of their time regarding advanced concepts in the planning and design of such facilities. Many of those buildings still remain, but they are not accessible to the general public.

NEW D.L.&W. LOCOMOTIVE SHOPS
SCRANTON PA.
VIEW FROM PASSENGER STATION 5.14.10

D.L.&W.
#B.676.

The locomotive shops at the Delaware, Lackawanna & Western Railroad were supplied with water gas, a hot, even-burning artificial gas that was manufactured on-site by the DL&W from its own supply of anthracite. This c. 1910 photograph was taken from the Lackawanna Passenger Station.

A new concrete oil house began construction just west of the roundhouse in 1911 and was completed in 1912. The purpose of the oil house was to store the yard's flammable lubricants and lighting fluids. Tanks with larger quantities of oil were stored belowground in the concrete basement for safety. During the steam era, railroads across the nation constructed oil houses for this very reason. The original building remains on the site today and is utilized as a museum shop/bookstore on one side with an exhibit of the restored pump room on the other.

The old DL&W passenger station was demolished in 1909. It had stood for nearly 40 years. During all that time, it provided the city and its people with ample railroad services. All that remained was a shell of the former Victorian brick structure.

The Railroad YMCA restaurant, which also served as an official clubhouse, was located at 55 Lackawanna Avenue. Many railroaders spent a night or two and enjoyed a hot meal there for decades. With the decline of the railroad industry in the 1960s also came the demise of the Railroad YMCAs across the country.

Here is a view of the freight house yard. Note the Scranton House in the foreground. A well-known establishment in the early 1900s, it had rooms for 40 patrons and was on Lackawanna Avenue, not far from the DL&W yard.

The office and storage building at the South Washington Avenue entrance was connected by subways, or underground tunnels, to the former Scranton Army Ammunition Plant, which was once owned by the Delaware, Lackawanna & Western Railroad company. Their construction was a significant element of the DL&W's 1898–1925 modernization program. Many of the tunnels remain today but are closed to the public.

Pictured is the demolition of the old shops once located near the South Washington Avenue entrance to the yard. This area of the yard, including what is today the Scranton Police Station, was once called Hogtown and was where the original roundhouse and turntable were in the 19th century. During that time, small switch locomotives and engineers were called hogs. Pictured is the toppling of the old stack.

Seen in this c. 1913 photograph is the boiler of the first locomotive built in Lackawanna's new shops—a momentous occasion.

In 1907, the track on the north side of the yard was widened and elevated for DL&W's passenger line. A derailment occurred that same year. Railroad accidents were very common at the time. One of the worst rear-end collisions on the DL&W line was the Gibson train wreck, which occurred on July 4, 1912, in Corning, New York. Thirty-nine passengers lost their lives, including several Scrantonians, and eighty-six were injured.

Ground was broken for the new station on September 1, 1906, at the opposite end of Lackawanna Avenue from the original brick building due to the shifting of the city's business district. After a suitable lot was chosen, a competition was held for selecting the building's architect. Kenneth Murchison, a New York architect, was chosen. Murchison was known for designing train stations. Construction cost over $500,000, and upon completion, a majestic iconic building enriched the city.

The 240-foot-by-88-foot station consisted of a frame of steel and brick. Its French Renaissance architectural style, with six columns adorning the front entrance, welcomed weary travelers. On the track side, train sheds with steel trusses, concrete roofs, and skylights allowed passengers comfort as they waited for their trains. On the first floor was a newsstand, telegraph office, ticket office, mail room, and baggage area, plus a lunchroom so that a passenger could enjoy a bite to eat before boarding. It also housed offices for freight claim, auditing, and additional departments, including the station master's office and record room.

The new Delaware, Lackawanna & Western station was dedicated on November 11, 1908. DL&W officials from New York, headed by President Truesdale, arrived in Scranton for the celebration. Today, the building houses the Radisson Lackawanna Station Hotel, and is still a majestic sight upon entering the heart of the city.

Here is the luxurious office of a DL&W official in the Lackawanna passenger station. An additional floor was added to the station to house the offices of railroad executives.

Pictured are a few of the men who worked on the passenger station. People of all ethnicities worked side by side in order to promote the growth of the city.

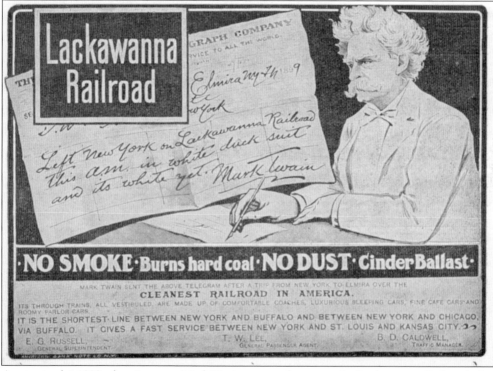

As seen in this 1899 advertisement, Mark Twain sent a telegram to the Lackawanna Railroad after a trip from New York to Elmira. "Left New York on Lackawanna Railroad this morning in white duck suit and its white yet." The ad boasted the Lackawanna as the cleanest railroad in America.

The DL&W mascot, Phoebe Snow, was featured in a magazine ad campaign that proclaimed that the DL&W, which burned hard anthracite coal, was less likely to leave a coating of coal dust on passengers' clothes. Phoebe, who always wore spotless white linen, was created by advertising agency Calkins and Holden. Some 60 poems were written for the ad campaign, such as "Says Phoebe Snow / About to go / Upon a trip / To Buffalo: 'My gown stays white / From morn / till night / Upon the road of anthracite.'" Within the first 10 years of the campaign, the number of DL&W passengers increased by 80 percent. The original ad ran from 1900 until World War I. Phoebe took center stage again from 1949 to 1967, when the DL&W introduced a new train named in her honor. People often ask if Phoebe Snow was a real person, but she was fictional—well, mostly. Her face and figure were inspired by model and actress Marion Murray.

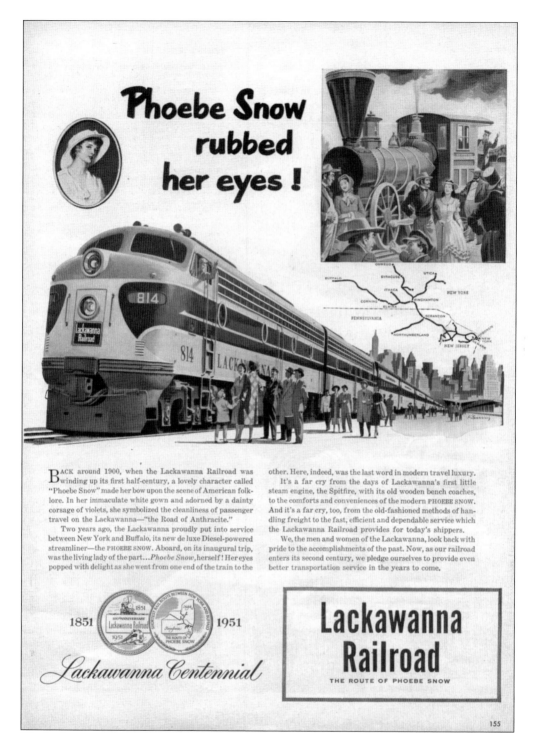

Phoebe Snow rubbed her eyes!

BACK around 1900, when the Lackawanna Railroad was winding up its first half-century, a lovely character called "Phoebe Snow" made her bow upon the scene of American folklore. In her immaculate white gown and adorned by a dainty corsage of violets, she symbolized the cleanliness of passenger travel on the Lackawanna—"the Road of Anthracite."

Two years ago, the Lackawanna proudly put into service between New York and Buffalo, its new de luxe Diesel-powered streamliner—the PHOEBE SNOW. Aboard, on its inaugural trip, was the living lady of the part...*Phoebe Snow*, herself! Her eyes popped with delight as she went from one end of the train to the other. Here, indeed, was the last word in modern travel luxury.

It's a far cry from the days of Lackawanna's first little steam engine, the Spitfire, with its old wooden bench coaches, to the comforts and conveniences of the modern PHOEBE SNOW. And it's a far cry, too, from the old-fashioned methods of handling freight to the fast, efficient and dependable service which the Lackawanna Railroad provides for today's shippers.

We, the men and women of the Lackawanna, look back with pride to the accomplishments of the past. Now, as our railroad enters its second century, we pledge ourselves to provide even better transportation service in the years to come.

1851 *Lackawanna Centennial* **1951**

Lackawanna Railroad
THE ROUTE OF PHOEBE SNOW

155

The Lackawanna railroad introduced a diesel-powered streamliner named the *Phoebe Snow* in 1949. This ad compares the comfort and convenience of the modern locomotive to Lackawanna's first steam engine, the *Spitfire*. In its later years, the *Spitfire*, seen at top right, was used as a switcher before being scrapped in 1885. (Courtesy of D.M. Crispino.)

A fire occurred on September 13, 1917, in the roundhouse at the DL&W yard between Washington Avenue and Cliff Street. The fire started in the southeast portion of the building. It was discovered by a citizen about 7:00 p.m., and the alarm on the street box was sounded. It took the firemen about 90 minutes to get the fire under control due to low pressure in the water supply. The cause of the fire was determined to be spontaneous combustion. About 21 engine stalls were destroyed and property loss totaled $15,000. Fortunately, there were no fatalities.

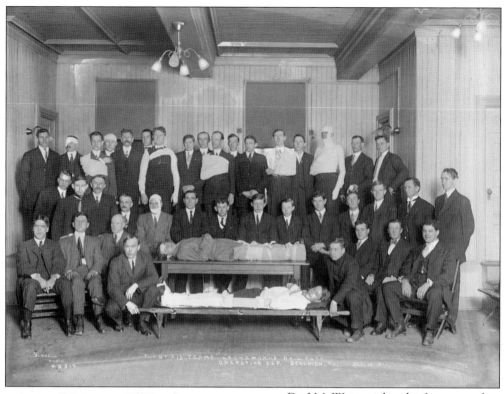

It sure is a cat-
astrophe when
anyone gets hurt

Dr. J.M. Wainwright, chief surgeon of
the DL&W railroad, was quoted in *Red
Cross* magazine saying there would be
beneficial results from the knowledge of
first aid among the railroad employees.
Many of the Lackawanna Railroad
employees were trained in first aid,
not just to help injured coworkers but
also to help people in various towns
the Lackawanna served. Pictured
above is the 1917 first aid team of the
Lackawanna Railroad. The safety ad at
left is from the *Lackawanna Supervisor*,
a publication for DL&W employees.

During the early 1900s, the DL&W completed two notable projects that greatly improved operations: the New Jersey cutoff (Port Morris, New Jersey–Slateford, Pennsylvania) and the Nicholson-Hallstead cutoff. This magnificent feat of engineering produced several reinforced concrete viaducts. The best known was the Tunkhannock Viaduct, also known as the Nicholson Viaduct (pictured). It still stands today and is a sight to behold, especially with "Lackawanna R.R." across the center arch.

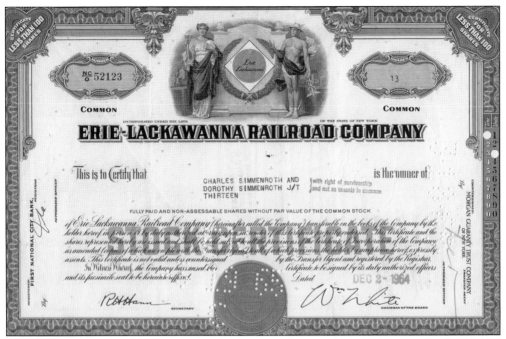

By 1950, the diesel locomotive introduced 20 years earlier was the way to go. Sadly, the DL&W deemed its steam facilities obsolete. The railroad industry had a hard time competing with highways, airplanes, and waterway transport. On the verge of bankruptcy, the DL&W merged with its rival, the Erie, and the name was changed to the Erie Lackawanna Railroad.

This is the DL&W yard as it looked from above in 1951. Even after its merger with the Erie Railroad, financial issues worsened as passenger train service continued to deteriorate. In 1976, the Consolidated Rail Corporation (Conrail) was formed through the merger of numerous railroads, including the now bankrupt Erie Lackawanna. The Scranton yard was then deeded to Conrail.

Two

THE MAN, THE MOGUL

Francis Nelson Blount (left)
and his childhood friend
Frederick Richardson (right)
wrote a book titled *Along
the Iron Rails* when they
were teenagers out of their
love for steam locomotives.
Blount went on to become
a millionaire before the age
of 30 due to his successful
seafood corporation, but he
never lost his passion for
steam power locomotives. His
lifelong ambition had been to
become a railroad engineer
and to own a railroad, and
now, he had the financial
means to achieve both.

After passing a test to become an engineer for the Boston & Maine, Blount purchased the narrow-gauge Edaville Railroad in South Carver, Massachusetts, in the mid-1950s. Blount served as president, and Fred Richardson was vice president. Even though he now owned a narrow-gauge railroad, he longed to have a standard-gauge road and began acquiring many standard-gauge locomotives and railroad cars. Blount is pictured in the cab of No. 89 talking with visitors.

As his collection of standard-gauge locomotives continued to grow, Blount found he needed a new location to store them. In 1960, he purchased the terminal facilities of the Boston & Maine in North Walpole, New Hampshire. Here, he displayed his collection and also started an excursion line for tourists.

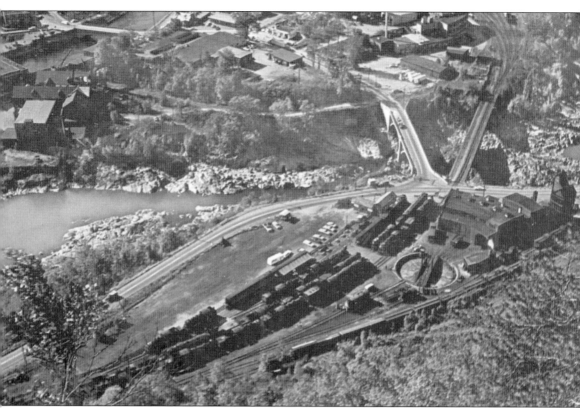

Four years later, Blount bought the Rutland track rights between North Walpole and Westmore, New Hampshire, just two miles north in Bellows Falls, Vermont, where he relocated his collection once again. His purpose in purchasing the Rutland tracks was to operate excursion runs and a year-round freight-passenger line. The excursion trains ran out of four different locations: Sunapee, New Hampshire; North Walpole, New Hampshire; Keene, New Hampshire; and Bellows Falls, Vermont. Steamtown, USA was born.

Three Steamtown, USA employees are standing in front of the yardmaster office. The job of the yardmaster was to review train schedules and switching orders, as well as coordinate the activities of the workers engaged in railroad traffic operations.

The Union Pacific No. 4012 4-8-8-4 "Big Boy" was the star of Steamtown, USA. Blount paid $6,000 to have it transported from the Union Pacific yards in Iowa to his Vermont site.

Two blasts from the past are seen here in one photograph. Collecting vintage automobiles was another of Blount's many hobbies.

Here is the Steamtown, USA directory. Blount's train museum had become a successful tourist attraction. The number of daily visitors to the museum increased substantially through the mid-1960s.

The beautiful countryside of Bellows Falls, Vermont, during autumn is seen here. People clamored to buy tickets for a train ride to see the vibrant foliage. The trains ran from late May through October. Blount had many plans for Steamtown, one of which was the addition of a side-wheeler steamboat, but fate would unfortunately intervene.

Tragically, on August 31, 1967, at the age of 49, Nelson Blount was killed when the plane he was piloting crashed into a large pine tree in Marlborough, New Hampshire. Due to the suddenness of his death, no arrangements had been made for the future of Steamtown, USA. The collection he took great pride in was now in danger of being sold.

To make matters even worse, in 1970, Vermont passed air-quality regulations that prohibited the site from using steam locomotives. Diesels took the place of steam power for the Steamtown, USA excursions, and ticket sales fell dramatically.

Blount's death presented many challenges for the remaining trustees of the Steamtown Foundation for years. In a last-ditch effort to bring Blount's boyhood dream back to life, Steamtown's equipment received much needed repairs. But the lack of funds was still the biggest problem in keeping the museum operating.

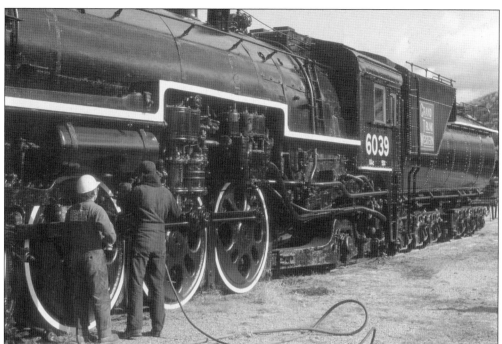

Workers in Vermont are using an airgun to shoot alemite grease into the drive box around the axle of the Grand Trunk Western No. 6039.

A crew member at Bellows Falls is seen lettering one of the Central Railroad of New Jersey trains. This task takes a very steady hand.

Fred Richardson and others worked to produce a film that focused on the life of Nelson Blount. It was a well-received tribute to the man's remarkable career.

Despite the trustees' efforts since Blount's death to save his train museum, by 1983, Steamtown, USA was in deep financial trouble. Don Ball, Steamtown's director at the time, had hoped the state's tourism officials would take more interest in promoting a museum with the world's largest collection of steam-powered railroad equipment. Unfortunately, they did not. The trustees were convinced that the location was also part of the problem, because they were too far from a populated city. The search for a new location had begun.

The ruins of Steamtown in Bellows Falls, Vermont, once a dream of F. Nelson Blount, are pictured here. The museum was now a vague memory, but Blount's legacy would live on.

The sign says it all. It may have been the end of one chapter, but it was only the beginning of a new one.

It has been said that if Blount's entire collection was placed end to end, it would be nearly two miles long. The Union Pacific No. 737 4-4-0, built by Baldwin in 1887, was the old-timer of the Bellows Falls Steamtown collection.

Aside from the Monadnock Northern No. 2, Blount owned many famous locomotives. One pulled Pres. Franklin Roosevelt's train from Massachusetts to Maine for a meeting with Winston Churchill, and another was previously owned by Barbara Guggenheim, the copper heiress.

Canadian Pacific 4-6-2 No. 1246 was built in 1946 by the Montreal Locomotive Company. No. 1246 was still in service at Bellows Falls during its last season in 1983, on runs called the "Farewell to Vermont" excursions. Ironically, its last season was one of its most successful in many years.

The Steamtown, USA 4-6-2 No. 127 was refurbished by Blount in 1964 and was used all over New England for his "Steam Safari" excursion. It was built in 1948 and was still considered mint condition in 1964.

The Southern Railway 4-4-0 No. 926 was built at Eastleigh, England, in 1934. Engines in this class were named after preparatory schools. This one was named the *Repton*. Blount had it shipped from England to Montreal. From there, it was towed to Vermont and added to his growing collection.

The Canadian National 4-6-2 No. 5288 was a typical heavy passenger locomotive of the Roaring Twenties. It could be seen all over North America pulling mail, passenger, and Pullman cars. No. 5288 was built in 1919 by the Montreal Locomotive Company.

In the 1970s, the Canadian Pacific 4-6-4 No. 2816 was one of the few Hudson engines left in North America, since no others had been preserved.

Eastern Gas and Fuel Co. No. 4 was the biggest 0-6-0 ever delivered in New England when it left the Baldwin Works in Philadelphia in 1911. The switch engine went to work for the New England Gas & Coke Co. near Boston. before retiring to Blount's Steamtown.

The Belgium State Railways 0-4-0 No. 3364 was the oldest engine at Blount's Steamtown. It was built in 1877 and used for switching around a coal mine in Belgium. The No. 3363 was able to run at a speed of 20 miles per hour.

Three

THE NATIONAL
HISTORIC SITE

The decaying former DL&W rail yard had become overgrown with weeds and rusted trains. It had been years since the sound of a train whistle had come from the now-abandoned ghost yard. In the early 1980s, a syndicated column featured in the *Scranton Times* asked if any old railroad towns would be interested in having the Bellows Falls collection. Many in Scranton answered with a resounding, "Yes!"

Moving Steamtown, USA from Vermont to Scranton would take several years. The process began with the City of Scranton obtaining the deed for the old rail yard from Conrail. Scranton mayor James McNulty pledged $2 million over a three-year period to finance the move.

Scranton welcomed Steamtown, USA on February 4, 1984, when Canadian Pacific No. 2317 pulled six passenger coaches filled with dignitaries and officials to the Hilton at Lackawanna Station. It was greeted by an estimated crowd of 10,000, shouting and snapping pictures. Operations began on September 1 that same year using the No. 2317, and later adding the Canadian Pacific No. 1246 to the daily schedule of train rides.

A portion of the site is seen from what is today the Lackawanna County Transit Center. The building in the foreground is the future home of the Lackawanna County Electric City Trolley Museum. Through the years, the building was home to many businesses and warehouses, including the United Silk Mill and William's Bakery.

Here is the Nickel Plate Road No. 759 in the early 1980s. At the time the photograph was taken, the Scranton Dry Goods and Casey Hotel were still part of the city's skyline.

Even though the buildings are no longer owned by the Delaware, Lackawanna & Western Railroad, signs for the erecting shop and other Lackawanna Railroad locomotive shops can still be seen.

Sadly, the last passenger train pulled out of the station on January 5, 1970. The abandoned passenger station was renovated as a hotel in the early 1980s in hopes of attracting tourists to the economically flailing city. The building was renamed the Hilton at Lackawanna Station and had a grand opening on New Year's Eve 1983. It remained a Hilton until 1995.

Who is going to win the race, the Canadian Pacific No. 2317 or the Delaware & Hudson No. 4075? The No. 2317 was the first Steamtown, USA locomotive to move to Scranton.

This is the return of the first train trip from Pocono Summit to Scranton. Pictured is Ron Fimbleton. The first season of Steamtown had used the Hilton at Lackawanna Station as a boarding site.

Just north of the Route 507 crossing, the Lackawanna No. 54 along with coaches Nos. 717, 1022, 1006, 1026, and 589 can barely be seen through the cloud of smoke they leave in their wake on one of the excursions. At first, the future of Steamtown in Scranton looked bright, but like Bellows Falls, the lack of financial support to keep up with expenses would put it once again on the brink of bankruptcy. Pennsylvania congressman Joseph M. McDade would lend a helping hand.

Here is a scene from a railfan weekend in 1986. Excited train enthusiasts are delighted to get a close-up look at the Rahway Valley No. 15 (left) and the Canadian Pacific No. 2317 in the rear of what was once the Lackawanna Passenger Station. That same year, on October 30, the once privately owned Steamtown, USA became the Steamtown National Historic Site. It would not officially open for another two years.

This is the Grand Trunk Western No. 6039 being brought into Scranton with some help from its friends around 1987.

Early on, there was a lot of work to be done to refurbish the site so that tourists would be able to appreciate the beautiful trains such as the Canadian Pacific No. 2317.

This was a test run of Lackawanna No. 2317 for the Pocono Mountain Route in the yard. Members of the Steamtown crew are cleaning out the ashes. It is important to perform daily routine maintenance on steam locomotives. During the 1986 season, the Canadian locomotive went back into excursion service. Its tender was lettered "Lackawanna," and the running board skirts read "Pocono Mountain Route."

Passengers are boarding a special tour train from Scranton to Pocono Summit in November 1987.

Electric City is seen from the yard. The Scranton Dry Goods, one of the city's oldest department stores, founded in 1892 as the Jonas Long and Sons Store, is seen in the background.

Pictured is the July 1, 1988, ribbon-cutting celebration for the official opening of the Steamtown National Historic Site. Congressman Joseph M. McDade is at center.

This is a view of the yard in 1988. Quite a challenge lay ahead for the National Park Service. Following the initial opening, much work and repairs were needed to restore the site to operational standards.

Construction of the new proposed complex began in the summer of 1991. It was a major undertaking that would take several years to complete. Two of the DL&W's original structures, the oil house and the 1902 roundhouse office, can be seen in the background. The roundhouse office is one of the oldest buildings on the complex. Renovation was planned for both structures.

At left above is a portion of the DL&W's second roundhouse, built in 1902. The building was part of a 46-stall roundhouse. After the modernization program, only three stalls remained from the 1902 design.

Here is the wooden frame of the excursion loading platform in the yard. Once completed, the visitors would gather here to board the train for a trip to Moscow, or one of Steamtown's longer excursions to the Delaware Water Gap.

By 1992, the turntable was coming along nicely. The hub of the roundhouse is considered the turntable; from it, tracks radiate like spokes into each stall of the roundhouse. The roundhouse was also being rehabilitated to allow Steamtown mechanics to maintain the locomotives. Much of the construction of the north exhibit building was concluded by the end of the year. Construction of the visitors' center and theater began in the summer of 1992 and was slated for completion in 1994.

Here is a glimpse of the nearly completed complex in 1994. The parking area was still in the beginning stages. A portion of the remnants of the former Dickson Locomotive Works was torn down to make room for the parking lot.

That same year, the restoration of the oil house was completed. The building has survived the test of time, having been one of the original structures built in 1912. Behind the building is a brick border marking the location of the foundation and cellar of an oil house built around 1870. This oil house was the earliest known oil storage and distribution facility at the DL&W yard.

Installation of the switch took place near the former Lackawanna Passenger Station. A railroad switch consists of a pair of rails that are linked to one another and guide a train from one track to another, such as at a railway junction.

The implosion of 24 buildings along the 300 and 400 blocks of Lackawanna Avenue occurred on April 5, 1992, to make way for the Steamtown Mall. It was quite a sight to behold from a safe distance. The architect was William Kessler, who was commissioned by Al Boscov, owner of one of the mall's anchor stores. The mall officially opened in October 1993.

A pedestrian bridge was built from the Steamtown Mall to the historic site so visitors could have easy access to both. It is located where the DL&W's coal dock once stood. A tourist can spend the day learning about railroad history and then enjoy a little shopping afterward.

Some final touches are done on the ticket booth and parking lot as opening day grows near. The visitors' parking lot is an expansive area. There are designated sections large enough to accommodate buses, motor homes, and towed trailers.

After many years of hard work and planning, the new complex included a visitors' center, two museums (technology and history), a theater, a restored operational roundhouse, and a new turntable. There is also a bookstore/museum shop in the original 1912 oil house. Opening day was scheduled for July 1, 1995. A celebration had been months in the making, with Ranger Tim O'Malley heading the Steamtown grand opening committee.

Pictured is the long-awaited grand opening on July 1, 1995. Pennsylvania governor Robert P. Casey sang some lyrics from an old Italian-American folk song: "Where do you work-a, John? / On the Delaware Lackawan'." An estimated 10,000–25,000 were in attendance. The highlight of the day was the Parade of Steam. Participating in the impressive lineup were the Baldwin 0-6-0 No. 26 (pictured below), Canadian National 2-8-2 No. 3254, and Canadian Pacific 4-6-2 No. 2317. Also participating were three guest locomotives, NYSW 2-8-2 No. 142, Reading, Blue Mountain & Northern 4-6-2 No. 425, and 4-8-4 Milwaukee No. 261. The ribbon-cutting ceremony was followed with speeches by various politicians.

Many events, like train trips to Moscow and night photograph sessions, had been planned for the three-day celebration. According to an article in *US News & World Report*, "Steamtown, which could have been the industrial equivalent of an elephant boneyard . . . will instead provide a fascinating and evocative experience when the park opens on July 1," and indeed, it has.

Pictured at right are, from left to right, Congressman McDade, park superintendent Terry R. Gess, and unidentified addressing the crowd on the "Big Boy." At 5:00 on the final day, three of the locomotives, including the Shay No. 8, blew their whistles simultaneously to conclude the celebration. The grand opening of the Steamtown National Historic Site was deemed a great success.

In 1996, one year after the opening of the newly built complex, visitation to Steamtown was still going strong. Whether tourists would return for repeat visits was never in question. Through the years, Steamtown has offered many different events to draw the public back, from visiting trains to the annual Railfest Weekend. The past never gets old at Steamtown.

From left to right, Joe Tully, Lori Staely, and Ron Scott say cheese for the camera. All of Steamtown's staff and volunteers are friendly and knowledgeable about the history of the site and its vast collection of trains and railroad artifacts.

At one time, the Dickson Locomotive Works occupied the area toward the west side of the former DL&W yard. Through research of historical documents, it is believed that both companies enjoyed an amicable business relationship.

This is the building that would become the Lackawanna County Electric City Trolley Museum, which is now the permanent home of John Oliver's model train, a gift to local television station WNEP 16.

Steamtown's neighbor across the parking lot is the Lackawanna County Electric City Trolley Museum. It had been slated to open in 1996, but because of several delays, it officially opened to the public in 1999. The museum was created by the Lackawanna Heritage Valley Authority.

Built in 1922, this DL&W boxcar has "Lackawanna, The Route of *Phoebe Snow*" painted on its side. It remained in service until the early 1950s. Boxcars were used to transport products and commodities that required protection from the elements or from breakage. The National Park Service acquired it in 1993 and restored it to how it looked in the 1950s. (Courtesy of Tim O'Malley.)

From left to right are John Rendle, Jerry Kuczynski, and Andrew Giardina. Some of the Steamtown shop crew are riveting sheets of steel together in crafting a cab for the cosmetic restoration of Bullard Machine No. 2. (Courtesy of Tim O'Malley.)

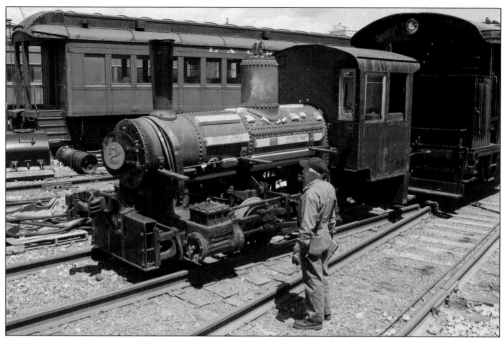

Another member of the crew, Paul Ratcliffe, is working on the Bullard Machine No. 2, Steamtown's smallest locomotive. (Courtesy of Tim O'Malley.)

The rear of the Steamtown Mall, now called the Marketplace at Steamtown, occupies the area of the former DL&W main line, known as the "China Wall." This fill brought the passenger tracks up to the station.

This is a night photograph session during one of Steamtown's World War II commemoration weekends in 1998. The models had to stand perfectly still for three minutes while the organizer of the photo shoot ran around the scene painting it with flashbulb light. (Courtesy of Tim O'Malley.)

Steamtown National Historic Site superintendent Kip Hagen welcomes visitors at the 10th anniversary of the museum complex opening on July 1, 2005. (Courtesy of Tim O'Malley.)

This c. 2016 photograph was taken to commemorate the 50th anniversary of the signing of the National Historic Preservation Act. The theme was "Hug Your History." The children with Ranger Dan Kahl are from Evergreen Elementary School in Hamlin, Pennsylvania. They are hugging Berlin Mills Paper Company No. 7. (Courtesy of Tim O'Malley.)

Every year, the Steamtown National Historic Site delights children of all ages with the "Santa Train." Santa and Mrs. Claus are greeted with smiling crowds and cheers at every stop. The annual event begins in Carbondale and then heads south as children await St. Nick at the last stop, the core complex of Steamtown. (Courtesy of Tim O'Malley.)

The Union Pacific No. 4012 4-8-8-4 steam locomotive, also known as the "Big Boy," was built by the American Locomotive Works in November 1941. Known for being the most powerful locomotives ever made and designed for hauling wartime freight and troop trains over the Rocky Mountains, their weight alone is staggering at 1.2 million pounds. The total length of engine and tender is 132 feet, 9.875 inches. It was built to achieve 80-mile-per-hour speeds. There were 25 made, and only eight are left in existence. No. 4012, on display at the Steamtown National Historic Site, is the only one on the East Coast.

The Canadian National Railways No. 3254 was built in 1917 by the Canadian Locomotive Company. The 2-8-2 Mikado was used on government railways for a brief time. The No. 3254 was built to pull freight trains. The operational history of this class of Mikado is unknown. Upon its arrival in Scranton, the Steamtown Foundation lettered its new locomotive "Lackawanna" in honor of the defunct railroad and gave it the fictional No. 1271.

H.K. Porter Company of Pittsburgh, Pennsylvania, built the Bullard Company 0-4-0T No. 2. It was purchased by Nelson Blount in 1963 from the American Machinery Corp. The Bullard is one of the smallest standard-gauge locomotives built.

At one time, the Boston & Maine 4-6-2 No. 3713 was named the *Constitution* during a contest run by the railroad. This locomotive was sold to Nelson Blount in 1960 and is part of the original fleet at the Steamtown National Historic Site. The Boston & Maine was used in passenger and fast freight service and is the only survivor of the series No. 3710–3714, class P-4-a.

The Brooks-Scanlon Corp. 2-6-2 Prairie-type No. 1 locomotive was another in Nelson Blount's collection, which he purchased in 1967. It was built by the Baldwin Locomotive Works in 1914 and sold to Brooks Scanlon Corp. in 1917. The No. 1 has the capability to burn either coal or wood. It is the only 2-6-2-wheel arrangement in the Steamtown collection.

The Canadian National 4-6-4T No. 47 is the only Baltic tank locomotive in the United States, which is why Nelson Blount added it to his fleet in 1959. It was originally built for the Grand Trunk Railway Co. of Canada as No. 1542, but after a merger in 1923, it was renamed. Pictured are, from left to right, Canadian National No. 3377, Canadian National No. 5288, Canadian National No. 47, Canadian Pacific No. 2929, and Canadian Pacific No. 1246.

The Maine Central 2-8-0 No. 519 engine is one of two remaining steam locomotives from that railroad. Built by ALCO in 1910, it spent most of its time on the rails in freight service. Nelson Blount purchased No. 519 in 1963. It is the second-most powerful 2-8-0 among the four of its type in the Steamtown collection.

The Lowville & Beaver River 2-8-0 Consolidation-type No. 1923 locomotive was built by the American Locomotive Company in October 1920. Three years later, the company sold it to Lowville & Beaver Railroad in New York, an Adirondack short line that hauled both passengers and freight. But first the American Locomotive Company had to remove the oil burner from its firebox and the oil tank from the tender. Also, the grates needed to be converted to coal fire. In June 1964, it was sold to Nelson Blount.

The Grand Trunk Western 4-8-2 No. 6039 was one of five in the 60376041 series, GTW class U-l-c. It was purchased for passenger service but could also be easily adapted to haul freight. It was leased to the Central Vermont Railway and sold to Nelson Blount in 1959. No. 6039 is one of fourteen 4-8-2s remaining in the United States and the only Mountain-class locomotive in the Steamtown lineup.

The Illinois Central 2-8-0 No. 790 was built by the American Locomotive Co. in November 1903. When it was sold to the Illinois Central Railroad in 1904, it became No. 641. In 1918, it was rebuilt as a heavy freight locomotive and renumbered to 790. Blount purchased it from a private owner in 1966; it is one of nine surviving from the Illinois Central Railroad.

Vulcan Iron Works built this standard-gauge 2-4-2T saddle tank switching locomotive; there are only two left in existence today. The Vulcan Iron Works was in Wilkes Barre, Pennsylvania, not far from Scranton. The No. 7 was sold to Groveton Paper Co. in New Hampshire in 1944, and then to the Berlin Mills Railway. Later, it was donated to Nelson Blount in 1969. Today, the Berlin Mills Railway No. 7 greets people at Steamtown's visitors' center.

The Rahway Valley 2-8-0 No. 15 was built as No. 20 for the Oneida & Western Railroad in Tennessee. It was used for hauling coal and lumber. It was purchased by the Rahway Valley Railroad and renumbered to 15. Nelson Blount purchased the No. 15 in 1959, and it remained in operation until 1973.

The E.J. Lavino Steel Co. 0-6-0T No. 3 is another from Nelson Blount's fleet. The American Locomotive Company built it in August 1927. It was outshopped as the Poland Springs Railroad No. 2. The history of this engine is a little uncertain. Records do not show if Poland Springs had possession of the engine or if it or Alco sold it to E.J. Lavino Steel in Sheridan, Pennsylvania, sometime between 1927 and 1949.

The Reading Company 4-8-4 No. 2124 is one of only nine remaining of the Reading Company locomotives. It was originally built by Baldwin as a 2-8-0 between 1923 and 1925. In 1947, it was rebuilt by the Reading Company as a 4-8-4 class T-1 Northern. This heavy freight engine was used in the Reading Company's "Reading Rambles" excursions.

The fireless locomotive was built for the Public Service Electric Company and was known by its builder's number, which was No. 6816, because the Newark Company never assigned it an engine number. These types of locomotives did not carry fuel or water but were instead charged with steam through a connection to a stationary steam boiler. The Public Service Electric & Gas Co. 0-6-0F No. 6816 was donated to the Steamtown Foundation in 1974.

The New York, Chicago & St. Louis Railroad (Nickel Plate Road) 2-8-4 No. 759 was from a large group of freight Berkshires built by Lima Locomotive Works in 1944. These steam locomotives were fast and modern enough to compete with diesels. It was sold to Nelson Blount in 1962 before being leased to the High Iron Company from 1968 to 1972 for excursions. It returned to Bellows Falls three years later and was inoperable. Only 20 Berkshire-type locomotives remain in the United States today.

The Nickel Plate Road 4-6-0 No. 44 was built for the New York, Chicago & St. Louis Railroad as part of an order for 10 ten-wheelers numbered 40–49, class P. In 1929, it was sold to Dansville & Mount Morris Railroad and is one of two remaining engines from that railroad. Learning of its existence, Nelson Blount purchased it in 1963 for display at Bellows Falls. The DL&W 2-6-0 No. 565 (pictured below) was built by the American Locomotive Company in September 1908. In the late 19th and early 20th centuries, "Moguls" like the No. 565 were popular. In 1960, it was purchased for the New Jersey tourist railroad. It had several private owners before it came into the possession of the Steamtown Foundation. No. 565 is the only remaining DL&W locomotive in the Steamtown collection. (Both, courtesy of Marnie Azzarelli.)

Another Mogul was the Norwood & St. Lawrence 2-6-0 No. 210. It was built in 1923 and is manually fired with a second sand dome and an all-weather cab. The No. 210 was sold to a scrap yard in the 1950s and saved by Nelson Blount in 1965.

This saddle tank switcher was operated as New Haven Trap Rock 0-4-0T No. 43 for Blakeslee & Sons quarry company, located in New Haven, Connecticut. It was built in 1919 by Vulcan Iron Works and was retired in 1959.

The Meadow River Lumber Co. No. 1 two-truck Shay is the only geared locomotive in the Steamtown collection. It was built by Lima Locomotive Works in 1910. Shay-patent geared locomotives were typical of engines used on industrial railroads. Nelson Blount added the locomotive to his fleet in 1959. While in storage at Bellows Falls, it was heavily damaged by the building collapsing on it due to excessive snow on the roof.

The Baldwin Locomotive Works of Eddystone, Pennsylvania, built the 0-6-0 No. 8 in 1923 for Spang, Chalfont and Company of Etna, Pennsylvania. The locomotive was operated in the vicinity of Pittsburgh for nearly 41 years. It was eventually disassembled and put into storage in Clarks Summit, Pennsylvania. A private owner purchased the No. 8 in 1995 for the purpose of restoring it to nonoperating condition. The switcher-type steam locomotive arrived at the Steamtown National Historic Site on July 25, 1996. It is on display and provides a three dimensional look at how a steam locomotive works.

The Canadian Pacific Railway No. 2929 was built in 1938 by the Canadian Locomotive Company, Kingston Works. The 4-4-4 wheel arrangement was given the name "Jubilee" to mark the 50th anniversary of the inaugurations of transcontinental service. In June 1958, it ran between Montreal and Farnham. The following year, it was purchased by Nelson Blount and put on exhibit at Edaville.

The Canadian National 2-8-2 No.3377 was originally built as Canadian Government No. 2977 in 1919. This engine is similar to the No. 3254. It had the capability to haul long main line freight trains. No. 3377 is one of the two Mikado-type locomotives at Steamtown National Historic Site.

The Canadian Pacific Railway 4-6-2 No. 2317 became a part of Blount's collection in 1965, but it was not put into service until 1978, more than 10 years after his death. The No. 2317 arrived in Scranton on January 31, 1984. Several days later, on February 4, the crew of Steamtown got the No. 2317 steamed up so the public could witness its highly publicized "grand entrance" to the city. The following September, No. 2317 headed Steamtown's first excursion trip from Scranton to Elmhurst.

The Central Railroad Company of New Jersey Railway Crane No. 5 and Idler Gondola No. 92082 were built by the Bucyrus Company in 1918. These two have been together since the mid-1960s. They are used in Northeastern Pennsylvania train wreck service and have the capacity of lifting 150 tons. Around 1975, the Steamtown Foundation in Vermont purchased it from either a private owner or the railroad.

The New York, Chicago & St. Louis Railroad 0-4-4-0 No. 514 is still in service at the Steamtown National Historic Site. It was built by Electro-Motive Division, General Motors Corporation, in La Grange, Illinois, in 1958. It was owned by two different railroads before being purchased by Steamtown, USA in Scranton. The No. 514 is primarily used in excursions and switching service.

The Long Island Railroad Rotary Snowplow No. 193 was retired in 1965. But it worked on the rails for many years, having been built at Cook Locomotive and Machine Works in 1898. It was sold to the Steamtown Foundation in 1988 and was moved by Conrail to the Steamtown National Historic Site in July 1993.

The Delaware & Hudson Railroad snow flanger No. 36037 is used for snow removal. It is estimated to have been built before 1910. The Steamtown Foundation acquired the flanger between 1985 and 1987.

Lehigh Valley Railroad caboose No. 95003 was donated by Conrail in 1988 to Steamtown but did not arrive on the site until 1990. It was repainted two years later.

Lehigh & New England Railroad caboose No. 583 was made at the Reading Company shops during the equipment modernization period in 1937. This caboose is one of three sold by the Central Railroad of New Jersey to the Steamtown Foundation in 1975. The crew at the historic site repainted and correctly renumbered if from 580 to 583 in 1999.

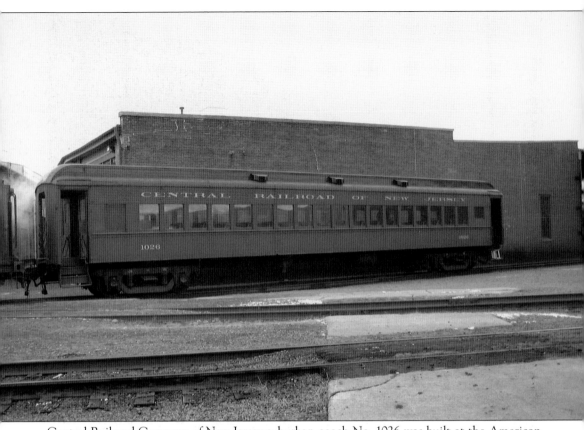

Central Railroad Company of New Jersey suburban coach No. 1026 was built at the American Car and Foundry in 1923. It was part of the 933–1168 series. These coaches were large enough to comfortably seat 78 passengers. In 1975, the Steamtown Foundation purchased the passenger cars. They arrived at the Scranton yard in the mid-1980s. The cars that are operational are still used today on the Steamtown National Historic Site's excursion train.

Delaware, Lackawanna & Western Railroad suburban coach No. 589 is another car used on the Steamtown National Historic Site's excursions. It is all steel, can seat 78, and was made by the Pullman Car Company in 1915.

The Rutland Railroad flatcar No. 2777 has a steel frame, stoke pockets, and a wooden deck. In 1989, the car was restored by Steamtown, where it is on display.

The Louisville & Nashville Railroad railway post office car No. 1100 was built by the American Foundry Company in 1914. This beauty was acquired by the Steamtown Foundation in 1977 and restored in 1999. The interior is intact and includes the folding and sorting tables and pigeonholes, which are still labeled from its last run. In 1965, the US Postal Service began to use airmail service more than the railway post office cars, marking the end of an era. The car is on display in the site's history museum.

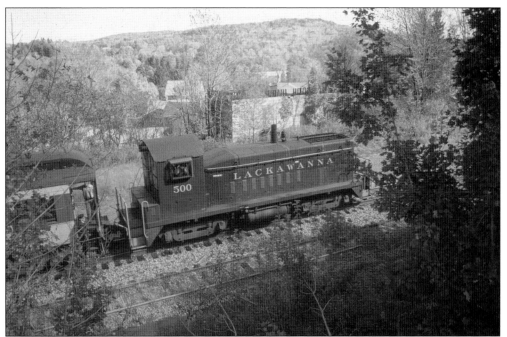

The Lackawanna No. 500 was built by the Electro-Motive Division, General Motors Corporation in LaGrange, Illinois, in 1953. This SW-8 800-horsepower diesel-electric locomotive was originally owned by the Wabash Railroad. In 1949, the company began replacing steam with diesel-electric locomotives. Very little information can be found on the SW-8 switching locomotive. It arrived at Steamtown in 1987, when the Steamtown Foundation repainted it to represent the Lackawanna colors and gave it the number 500. A locomotive with no historical connection to the Delaware, Lackawanna & Western Railroad would sometimes be given a fictional number and color scheme. Lackawanna No. 500 can be found in the Steamtown National Historic Site's yard.

The Baldwin Locomotive Works 0-6-0 No. 26 (left) is the only typical switch engine in the Steamtown collection. It was built in 1929. An estimated 112 0-6-0 switch engines with tenders like the Baldwin are all that remain in the United States. The No. 26 features a sloped-back tender. These locomotives mostly switched passenger and freight cars at major rail yards. The beloved Baldwin did not arrive at Steamtown National Historic Site until January 1990. Today, the Baldwin No. 26 is used for short train rides around the yard, which offer visitors a chance to view the former DL&W rail yard and imagine what it was like over a century and a half ago. On certain days, visitors can also take a longer trip on the little 0-6-0 to the tunnel of the Nay Aug Gorge. Pictured below with the Baldwin No. 26 is the Lackawanna No. 663. The DL&W-painted diesel locomotive is normally used for longer excursions to places like the Delaware Water Gap and Stroudsburg. Train rides at the Steamtown National Historic Site begin at the start of National Park Week during late April.

Then and now, beginning with the Delaware, Lackawanna & Western Railroad years, through steam and diesel, from Vermont to Scranton—the past is always present at the Steamtown National Historic Site. (Below, courtesy of Tim O'Malley.)

Discover Thousands of Local History Books Featuring Millions of Vintage Images

Arcadia Publishing, the leading local history publisher in the United States, is committed to making history accessible and meaningful through publishing books that celebrate and preserve the heritage of America's people and places.

Find more books like this at
www.arcadiapublishing.com

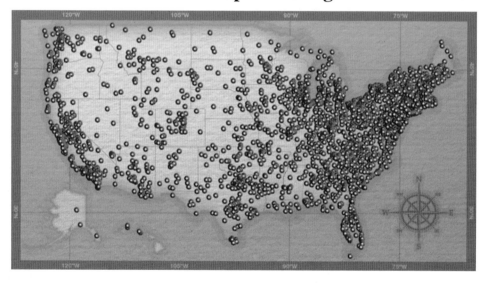

Search for your hometown history, your old stomping grounds, and even your favorite sports team.